This is not...
A Tourist Guide

21
CURIOUS PLACES
IN THE WORLD

Oriol Font i Bassa

in collaboration with
Albert Rubio Costa

Translated by Damian Nari

Spanish Edition: May 2020
Catalan Edition: July 2020
English Edition: September 2020

IN CASE YOU LIKE READING THE INDEXES

JUST AN INTRODUCTION,
SO IT IS NOT SO COLD

Dear reader...

Greeting is important. Always. It isn't difficult and you look good, you make the other person feel important, that you take them in consideration. And since we're going to be together for a while (I mean if you finish the book), that's how we experience a good start.

Well, dear reader: a few years ago, a friend (or someone who I thought that was my friend) recommended me, as a great masterpiece, that I see the movie The Rocky Horror Picture Show (a mix between Frankenstein, Terrifyingly Dead and a concert of Kiss). And I saw it. Entirely. From beginning to end. I fought not to fall asleep, but I finished it. The next day I told him that I had not liked it and he confessed that he used it for naps and that it had never passed the twentieth minute.

I know, you think this is not important, but you will understand.

Let's go back … Dear reader: if you have come to these pages, whether digital or on the classic 115 gram paper, looking for a tourist guide to visit some of the most curious places in the world, our short but intense friendship has reached this point. And I tell you like this, from the outset, so that we get along.

I do not offer you how to get there or where to stay or an amplified detail of everything you will find in each place. Nothing further. What you will find in this book is the wisdom of a pub, a chat, an afternoon gathering to leave your new diners speechless about how much you know, and to tire your old friends with more completely unnecessary information that fill that space you have between ears, there, just behind the eyes.

Some of the pearls you will be able to read in this book are about gardens that kill, craters that have been burning for fifty years because someone set them on fire, impossible roads, houses you would not want (or could not) live in or islands dominated by animals (and I don't mean very dumb people).

Do you feel like reading a bit, learning something and having some fun? Welcome. You have arrived to your Promised Land.

Oh, and if you have a little time to spare, preach the good news with your friends and make a review on Amazon, which is always helpful.

What don't you like? Recommend this humble work to those to whom you have no special devotion. Revenge and punishment, mixed with a bit of culture, are always more subtle and you make them waste their precious time more. Do you understand now about The Rocky Horror Picture Show?

If you feel like it, you can visit our website www.laisladelosconejos.com where you will find more curiosities of this planet that we exploit and that we call home.

PARTICULAR: if you are reading this book on paper format, do not try to click on the link on the web, it is useless. END OF SECTION.

Dear reader, welcome to 21 Curious Places in the World.

1.
WHEN HUMANITY PLAYS GOD

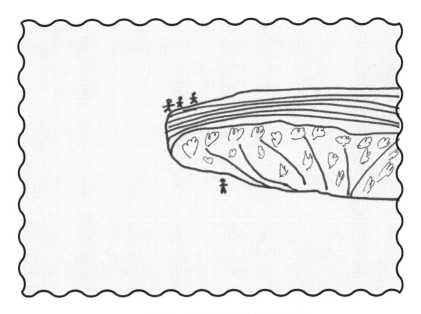

THERE IS NOTHING WORSE
THAN A VERY MOTIVATED USELESS

We all know that human imbecility can reach unsuspected heights, we just have to make a little effort
and we can achieve the most useless achievements
ever imagined. But it is also true that many times imbecility occurs without us, consciously, having put
ourselves to work to make happen any event worthy
of passing to the yearly Guinness Book of Records,
to zapping programs or to the urban legends that no
one would believe if they didn't know my mother's
neighbor's cousin.

There are some times when a spark jumps, when
our brain clicks (which I don't know if it's a temporal
connection or a too long disconnection from reality)

and we act in an unexpected, surprising and, without a doubt, completely out, by several meters, of all common sense or logical reasoning. Oh, a spark...

But before talking about the spark, if you allow me a small paragraph, I also say that the current idiot, and even the cohort of idiots who encourage him and feed his aspirations, at that moment they think that the idea that had his accidental idol is the best idea that has ever been on the earth.

We are going with the spark, but first, since I am here, I am going to make another small paragraph: these ideas have more presence with altered states of consciousness. Also when you are a child. But generally the imbecility is in the genes and is inherited.

THE RIGHT SPARK

As I said, there are times when there is a spark that jumps without us noticing and we manage to go down in history with an ¡Olé! at the full lungs of those who listen to our story. Because if we humans have something (especially the male gender) it is that we love to tell battles in which we are the protagonists, although these battles plunge us into the highest peaks of misery, as Groucho Marx would say. In the present case, the spark created a fire, and that fire has been burning for 50 years and no one knows when it will go out.

Let's get down to business: it was 1971, a team of Russian engineers and geologists were prospecting in the Karakum desert, in present-day Turkmenistan, when they accidentally drilled a cavern filled with gas. At one point, the ground collapsed under their feet, washing away machinery and equipment and leaving a crater 69 meters in diameter and 30 meters deep.

Up to this point, they are things that can happen... They shouldn't, but they can. Who has not sunk the typical tunnel that we made as children on the beach? So, what did you do? Well, you covered it and you were going to make another one. But there were also those who took advantage of the sinkhole to bury their sister up to his shoulders with the rising tide. Genius lurks in the most unexpected corners! And, in this case, it also made its stellar appearance.

Drum roll and... As going down there was dangerous, since gas kept coming out, they thought (think, why do people insist on thinking?) What they could do to recover the equipment that was at the bottom of the crater. One of the workers (presumably with a university degree under his arm and a doctoral gown from the former Soviet Union), had a great idea: he decided to set it on fire to burn all the gas and make it safe to go down.

Please, all together: Olé!

Now I'm going to do a bit of fiction literature, but I imagine all his colleagues, full of euphoria and the typical Russian tonic, encouraging that enlightened one, both by God and by the flame of his Zippo, to throw the lighter to the deep colossal hole.

THE COUNTRY'S TOURIST ATTRACTION

And it burned, well it did. The boy was not wrong, in fact, he erred on caution. Very cautious, I would say. And this happened in 1971. Today, the day these lines take shape, we are in the torrid month of July 2019, and the crater continues burning. Almost fifty years red hot, consuming the precious gas. And the worst, or the best depending on how you look at it, is that no one knows when it will stop burning, since Turkmenistan is home to one of the largest reserves of natural gas in the world.

But one thing must be granted to that useless motivated: he managed to include, even by force, the Karakum desert in all the tourist guides by building the well-known Hell Gate, one of the tourist attractions of the country and the silk road.

A GARDEN THAT CAN KILL YOU

Who has not gone through the field and has shouted and cursed when nettles have brushed his arm? Well imagine that, instead of a small rash, the plant that touched your skin could cause death. If nettles aren't fun, this would be less so. But if you dedicate yourself to cultivating these beautiful assassins ...

Black doors and skulls painted on them welcome you to this cozy botanical garden in Alnwick, in the north of England. It is the Poison Garden, which under the motto "These plants can kill" invites you to stroll through its rose gardens, its fields of cherry trees, the classic fields of English grass and for more than 100 plants that can literally fry you. Well, now that I notice it is not literal, it is rather metaphorical, but we understand each other ...

Where does this madness come from? Some data:

TIME FOR CURIOSITIES
- They have more than 600,000 visitors a year.
- The blame for all is the Duchess of Northumberland Jane Percy
- The duchess was between creating a garden of medicinal plants or one of plants that kill. Hard choise...
- The landscape architect Jacques Wirtz, who had worked in the Jardin des Tuileries in Paris and in the gardens of the residence of the President of France, was the first to plan the remodeling of the gardens.
- The gardens are at the foot of Alnwick Castle, where the first Harry Potter films were filmed.

AND NOW A LITTLE HISTORY

In 1995, Jane Percy became the Duchess of Northumberland, an English region that borders Scotland, after her husband's brother died unexpectedly.

PAUSE Unexpected death, inheritance and garden of poisons? The story begins well ...

Her husband, the duke, to keep the idle woman busy, told her to take care of the gardens, because they were so neglected. No expense spared, Jane Percy hired Jacques Wirtz and began the remodel. But she wanted something different from all the other gardens in England. The conversation with her husband must have been something similar to:

JANE PERCY
I want to do something different ...

DUKE
Very good...

JANE PERCY
Do you think it's OK? It's safe?

DUKE
Of course (he said as he folded the newspaper and took his tea)

JANE PERCY
I want it to have different plants from the rest of the gardens ...

DUKE
What do you want to put?

JANE PERCY
I dont know...

DUKE
The best roses?

JANE PERCY
No.

DUKE
Carnivorous plants?

JANE PERCY
Neither.

DUKE
Orchids?

JANE PERCY
Too seen.

DUKE
Bonsai?

JANE PERCY
They are gardens, not models!

DUKE
And so?

JANE PERCY
I have thought of plants that kill.

(The duke left the tea on the table, looked at it with fear and never tasted it again)

END

She did it being inspired by the Gardens of Padua that the Medici used to kill their enemies by planting skilled assassins. But she only wanted glamorous plants, with a story to tell: belladonna, hemlock, strychnine ... Great classics of poisoning in the great fictions of our history. She said it was to educate children.

Perfect. The question is: what exactly did she want to educate them on? In the art of killing?

Anyway, if you want a park to go on a picnic with the family, look for another one, this could be a bit indigestible.

A penultimate curious fact: the laurel bush can kill you.

And the last: we will also find cannabis, coca plants and other drugs. To educate, the Duchess also says ...

CURRENT MEGALYTIC MONUMENTS

After a sushi and a few beers with a friend who was a history teacher (we already know that teachers have a lot of vacations and the fact that it's a Thursday in July they don't care) he told me that one day in class, when they were studying the topic of Egypt, a student asked him if the pyramids had been made by aliens. He, following the canons of a good teacher, sat on the table and told them "I'm going to tell you the truth: when you have all the time in the world and you don't care about the death of slaves, you can build whatever you want." And there the question ended, it was a shame no one told him about Coral Castle, in Florida.

TOO MUCH FREE TIME

Edward Leedskalnin built this megalithic monument by himself, which he named Coral Castle, since it is made with limestone formed by coral. As a whole it weighs 1,000,000 tons, with massive stones of several tons.

It is said that he did it as a tribute to a love that had to return. Honestly, I have not seen it live, but in photographs. It is spectacular, really spectacular, but what is called beautiful ... Well, it is not. The truth. And I say, what if that supposed love one day came back, saw what his former lover was doing and turned around? And he there, building, and building, and building ...

But that is not the issue, let's get back to what concerns us.

Currently it is a tourist attraction, but Leedskalnin had always shrouded it in an aura of mystery, since he worked alone and at night, something that always helps to create myths and stories among your neighbors. Nor did it help the fact that when asked how he did it, he simply said, with an air of incorrigible smugness or perhaps good-natured humility, that he had discovered the ancient pyramids' secret to make stones weightless. And of course, much less help the few photos that there are of him working, where he is seen with a pine tripod as the only support; some chains hanging to hold the stones; and the weight of his person and his brute force to move the tons of limestone.

THE BLACK BOX

We know that the false documentary The Hidden Side of the Moon was its reference, but would Jordi Évole* and his screenwriters be inspired by this story to make the documentary (yes, it was false) about 23-F** and the famous black box?

What is the black box? The one on 23-F is a box that Juan Carlos I has on his table during the speech to dismantle the coup. In the case of Coral Castle, it is the fact that embodies the myth. In many of the few photographs of Leedskalnin working at Coral Castle, a black box is seen on top of the tripod that nobody knows how to explain what it is, but which has been speculated as to whether it could be some technological device that works as an antigravity creator that allows the weightless movement of the stones. Or maybe it was nothing ...

And if it is already expensive to build this amazing monument, what would you say about moving it several kilometers? Well he did too. Of course, alone and at night. Who gives more?

Maybe everything has a simple explanation, like the one about time and human lives that my friend the teacher told me, or maybe everything is different from how we want it to be. But the fact is that having done it is already a lot. Moving a million tons of stone by yourself and without heavy machinery ... How did he do it? Who knows...

*Jordi Évole: Spanish reporter
** 23-F: February 23, 1981 the day of the coup in Spain

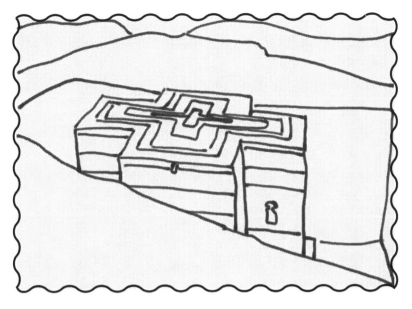

THE BLACK JERUSALEM

Tired of monoliths trying to reach the sky and blocks piled up in the shape of triangles? (I know that it is not the most exact definition of a pyramid, but we have understood each other, right?). Well, what would you think of 12 churches carved from a single block of hard rock each? You do not believe it? Well, when I talk to you about trips to heaven, angels working tirelessly in the style of slave exploitation and the Ark of the Alliance...

We traveled to Ethiopia, more specifically to Lalibela and its rock churches. For this, some data: the official language is Amharic, it occupies the world position number 15 in terms of population and 27 in terms of the country's surface, its highest point is Mount Ras Dejen

(4,553m), and the The majority religion is Christianity (Orthodox, Protestants and Catholics make up 63% of the population).

Having that said, we have always considered that Christianity came to Africa from the hand of the first Europeans who went with the mission of saving those savages from the eternal bonfire but that more than their souls what they wanted were their resources, but in Ethiopia It was not like this. In fact, it was the second country in the world to adopt the Christian faith, back in the 4th century, when Saint Frumencio of Tire baptized King Ezana.

And why is this data important? I like that you ask me this question. First, because a little general culture never hurts; and second, because the issue of religion is important in the story I'm going to tell you, the Lalibela: the Black Jerusalem.

WHAT IS LALIBELA?

Lalibela is a complex of 12 cave churches each excavated in a block of solid stone (basalt rock) that attempts to reproduce the city of Jerusalem. In 1978 they were declared a World Heritage Site by UNESCO (since then the tickets to visit them have progressively increased, reaching over € 50).

In the northern part we find the churches of Biet Medhani Alem (House of the Savior of the World), Biet Mariam (House of Mary), Biet Maskal (House of the Cross), Biet Denagel (House of the Virgin Martyrs), Biet

Golgotha Mikael (Gólgota House) and Biet Mikael (House of San Miguel); In the southeast, Biet Amanuel (House of Emmanuel), Biet Qeddus Mercoreos (House of San Mercurio), Biet Abba Libanos (House of Abbot Libanos), Biet Gabriel Rafael (House of Gabriel and Rafael) and Biet Lehem (House of Santo Pan). These two groups are separated by a water channel, the Yordamnos Channel, which represents the Jordan River. Away from the rest of the buildings, to the west, we find Biet Ghiorgis (House of San Jorge), the best preserved.

It is believed that they began by carving the ceiling, then the exterior walls and windows and, finally, they made the interior corridors and rooms. Can you imagine the pressure of building something like this? There is no place for mistakes, you cannot say "Oh, I was wrong, let's start again." It's a whole block of stone and there aren't many! They were not going to look for them in a quarry, they were there and they sculpted them, there could be no mistakes.

Between the different churches there are passageways or paths, also carved in the rock, that connect them.

HOW IS SOMETHING LIKE LALIBELA BUILT?
They were described for the first time by Francisco Álvares, a Portuguese priest who went to evangelize the country in 1520. Chronicles and drawings of the place are still preserved. History tells us that they were built by order of King Gebra Maskal Lalibela (around 1200) to represent the Holy Land, which had just been con-

quered by the Muslims. But what do historians and archaeologists tell us about the way they were built? Well, like all these great monuments, thousands of people did it over a long period of time. The pyramids, Stonehenge, Machu Picchu ... All these sites are outdoors, with plenty of space to come and go, the problem is that the narrow passageways that surround each building in Lalibela do not allow a large number of people to work ... And then appears myths and legends!

According to the local tradition, King Gebra Maskal Lalibela was led by God up to the heavens from where he showed him Jerusalem. Impressed by its beauty, he decided to make a replica in her country, Ethiopia. To help him, the Almighty sent a brigade of angels who worked during the day side by side with the inhabitants of that place. When humans slept, divine builders kept chipping stone (I don't know if noise would be easy to sleep with!).

It is unknown if those angels had done something wrong or did not like God, but if this is not angelic forced labor ...

The truth is that it is believed that many of the buildings were carved back in the 7th century as defensive fortifications or palaces of the dominant elite, so Gebra Maskal Lalibela only had to adapt them to his vision and build the rest. It was not little work either ...

THE ARK OF THE ALLIANCE
There are many theories that place the Ark of the Alliance in Africa, and one of them is the one that beli-

eves that it traveled to Ethiopia and was hidden in Lalibela. Yeah, yeah ... Why hasn't it been found? In fact, it is said that there is a room that only a chosen monk can enter. A monk who changes often due to premature deaths caused by cancer. It is speculated that it is due to the radiation that the Ark emits.

Another theory, somewhat far-fetched and perhaps meaningless, is that there is still a building to discover. We currently have 12, just like the apostles. Where is the house of Jesus? Shouldn't there be 13? It is believed that when it is found, the Ark of the Alliance will also be found inside.

Be that as it may, if you are in Ethiopia and you have € 50 in your pocket (something more because the guide also wants to charge and haggling is traditional but difficult), stop by Lalibela to see this marvel of engineering, be it divine or earthly.

2.
ISLANDS DOMINATED BY ANIMALS

THE ISLAND OF THE RABBITS

Konijneneiland, that's how the first European sett-
lers called an area, today a peninsula, once an island,
in the south of what we now know as Brooklyn. They
were Dutch and it meant Rabbit Island, because it was
infested with these animals. The name ended up de-
riving Coney Island and its habitants from fairground
specimens, from the strongest man in the world to the
bearded woman. But this is not the Island of Rabbits
that I want to tell you about.

The other Island of Rabbits, the one that concerns us
in this chapter, is Okunoshima. It is a small island of little more than 4 kilometers and that is located in the Seto
Inland Sea (Hiroshima Prefecture), in Japan. Thousands
of feral rabbits live there, chasing tourists in looking for

something to eat. Is this the great curiosity of the island? Well no, real curiosity is why they are there.

LET'S GO BACK A FEW YEARS

Okunoshima is an island far from any large population center and, therefore, the Japanese government used it to manufacture chemical weapons for World War II. Due to your great knowledge of the war history of different countries, I know what you are thinking, the same thing happened to me: but was not Japan one of the signatories of the Geneva Protocol that prohibited the use of this type of weapon? And yes, indeed you are not wrong, it was... But, oh those magnificent loopholes! The Geneva Protocol prohibited the use of chemical weapons, but did not prohibit their manufacture or storage.

Those human stupidities that we like so much ...

According to their spies, the United States and Europe were also manufacturing them, so they must have thought "Well, we will not be the only fools who for once do not look for the cracks in the laws and when they go crazy we will not have what to answer them with ...". And they got to work in 1929, although since 1927 the plant for this purpose was already being built.

The works and what was done there were surrounded by the highest Japanese secrecy, so much so that they even erased the island from many maps that existed at that time. The story could have been the following:

THE CAPTAIN OF THE SHIP:
Straight? But wasn't there an island around here?

NCO

In the navigation charts it says nothing ...

CAPTAIN

Well, I would swear there was an island... In fact, I think I'm seeing it.

(A Japanese Army ship approaches)

SERGEANT FOR THE MEGAPHONE

THERE IS NO ISLAND, YOU ARE IMAGINING IT. BUT THEY ALSO TURN THROUGH THEY CAN ENGAGE.

END

A KIND OF TRIBUTE TO THE VICTIMS

The fact is that even those who worked in the factory (with little protection and faulty safety suits) knew what they were doing. What caused illnesses in the short, medium and long term, so much so that the government ended up giving (not many years ago) aid to families so that they could cope with medical treatments.

At the end of World War II, the files that documented what was done there were burned, and the Allies disposed of the chemical weapons by dumping, burning or burying them (as always, if it is not seen, it is not there), and ordered to people to keep quiet about what had happened there.

But, apart from the human ones, there were other

victims: the rabbits that were used for the experiments that, once the factory was closed, were exterminated. It would have been nice to be able to say that some escaped and that their descendants now populate the Island of Rabbits, but no, they thoroughly exterminated them without leaving a puppet with a head, it was not the case that, due to what was done there, some had mutated and could tell the press about their experiences.

NOBODY ESCAPED

The rabbits that are there today were brought back together with the Okunoshima Poison Gas Museum, where they try to make people aware of the evils of war. A tribute to all the victims, human and rodent, that were there.

Without natural predators, the cute little animals reproduce with total impunity, handing out large family cards piecemeal and without worrying about whether they will find work or how they will pay for their studies. But there are some questions that remains:

How long will it take for the overpopulation of rabbits to decimate all natural resources and burden the island or suffer a gradual decline of pointed ears?

Do museum watchers do small nighttime exterminations to prevent over-spreading of long teeth?

Or maybe there is a population control with other less direct and more chemical methods? More than anything to continue with the tradition of the island ...

Questions that who knows if time will answer.

THE ISLAND OF THE SERPENTS

Albert Sánchez Piñol may have had evidence of this island or, at least, of the only inhabitant known in centuries, to write the novel Cold Skin. (SPOILER ALERT) The lighthouse keeper of an island where at night some aquatic humanoids come out of the sea in thousands to try to kill him. This was his story. The one that I want to tell you is the following:

An island of 430,000 m2 33 km off the coast of Brazil. Not far from Sao Paulo. There is a lighthouse that was automated since the beginning of the 20th century, leaving the poor lighthouse keeper who worked there unemployed. Damn technological evolution, always robbing us of the best jobs! I can imagine it: watch that the light is on and that it rotates. That's it, the rest of the time, go for a walk, eat, a coffee in the middle of the morning, a beer and a vermouth, read a little, write the same, a pajama nap and a potty... The dream job!

But when that man was there, he had to deal with something much worse than a bad internet connection, he had to deal with an island riddled with snakes of 30 different species. And not with four harmless little snakes that save you from putting rat killers to kill pests. No, that would have been too easy. To give an example: there is the *Bothrops insularis*, brownish in color, which can reach 70 centimeters in length and which holds the title of being one of the most poisonous snakes in the world. But not only that, to finish curling it, it is endemic to this island, so you cannot do anything to it because it is protected by international treaties.

The island I'm talking about is the Island of Queimada Grande, where the myth says that there are up to five snakes per square meter. False! The scientists proved that it was an exaggeration: there is only one for every square meter, so you still have room to put your feet...

POISON THAT HEALS

That said, it's a surpise that human presence on the Isle of Serpents is forbidden. But, as always, there are some exceptions, but they are few and far between. Let's be clear, as a paradisiacal tourist destination it doesn't sell much...

Only some scientific expeditions are allowed to enter the Island of Queimada Grande, after obtaining the necessary ophidian visas. And why would scientists want to go there? Well, to look for medicines. No, they are not the ones the lighthouse keeper left behind, they are the ones that our dragging friends can report to us.

And the fact is that the venom of Bothrops insulari, although it is one of the most dangerous in the world (it kills you in a few minutes), also harbors pleasant surprises: its poison, properly treated, is used in some medications for hypertension. If what doesn't kill you makes you stronger, what can kill you can also save you, always in the right measure, naturally.

LEGEND ALWAYS IMPROVES REALITY

Scientists tell us the history of this island as tectonic plates that move, a piece of land that is isolated along with the animals that lived on it, the evolution that goes by its side and creates endemic species... What always happens with the islands! Better a good story, right?

In some ancient writings they assure that the pirates landed on the island and buried succulent spoils from their comings and goings on the seven seas. And to keep them from strangers, they used neither money wells nor flood tunnels, they had already done that on Oak Island. No, the idea here to protect the treasures was to infest the island with poisonous snakes.

If it were true, the human stupidity that we love so much and that fills up millennia on YouTube would reappear.

What is certain is the visits of other pirates who currently visit the island: they are the poachers who risk their lives to obtain specimens of *Bothrops insulari*. Each of them can be worth 50,000 euros on the black market for animals.

Oh yeah. Wondering what snakes eat?Well, the Island of Queimada Grande is a stopping point and inn for many species of birds during their migrations. I suppose from year to year they don't remember what happened to their companions twelve moons before. It is that with time we only keep the good ...

THE ISLAND OF THE PIGS

The Bahamas, a paradisiacal destination for those dream vacations. White sand, blue waters, pigs swimming... Yes, as you hear it, pigs swimming. And no, I'm not talking about the pigs wearing sunglasses and swimsuits (usually leaving little to the imagination) that we can find in any public swimming pool sideways glancing at bikini-clad girls as they get out in the August sun. No, I mean real pigs swimming in the blue waters and wallowing on the white beaches.

This is what happens on Big Major Cay, in the Exuma district of the Bahamas. On this small wooded island, one of the 360 that we can find in the area, there lives a colony of about 20 feral pigs that have learned to swim. As you hear it. Why have they learned to swim? Well, out of necessity or, perhaps, to satisfy one of the most appetizing capital sins: gluttony. How do you satisfy this worldly pleasure? Exactly, swimming. Until where? Until the boats that approach its shores and give them a taste of delicate delicacies. Or maybe not so delicate ... Keep reading.

WHERE DID THEY COME FROM?

Nobody knows for sure where the first pigs that populated the island came from (to be clear, no humans live on the island, so when I refer to the pigs that populate the island, I mean that, pigs), but the human mind is rich with imagination and especially wild conspiracies and stories. And it is fortunate, but how would you fill in the following lines?

There are various theories and speculations: an oblivion, a misfortune or an advertising campaign. Yes, looking at it coldly, perhaps there are three misfortunes, but the fact is that there they are. Let's go with the first one.

The most widespread explanation is that, during colonial times, Dutch sailors left them on the island to keep them fresh so that they could eat them another day, but they never returned to collect them. Who knows if it was because of a mutiny on board that changed the course of the ship; an execution for a bad time desertion; or a simple shipwreck. The fact is that the legend says that they were left there and their descendants are still there.

Well, it could be, but imagine that you are starving after months at sea and you remember those pigs that you left on a remote island like an industrial refrigerator. Would you really like to have them hunt?

And since we were talking about shipwrecks, let's start with the second theory: a shipwreck is the one that took the pigs to the sea and, those who survived (that is, those who were lucky and knew how to swim) arrived on the island and made it their particular paradise.

In my opinion, this is the one I like the least, more than anything because it throws down the fact that they have learned to swim to get to the boats. But you are free to decide your favorite story and maybe this is it, everything can be.

But for me, the one that leaves me sleepless nights is the latter, the theory that I like the most: the pigs were put in by the rulers / businessmen of the Bahamas as part of a cunning plan to attract tourism to the area.

(PAUSE FOR REFLECTION)

Does anyone really believe that the Bahamas needs a few swimming pigs for tourism? I imagine the enlightened person on duty saying something like: "Yes, you'll see, we put pigs and teach them to swim. It's going to be amazing, then we filter it to the media and this is going to fill us with tourists ".

There are real marketing geniuses around the world!

FROM PARADISE TO HELL THERE ARE ONLY TWO YACHTS

Be that as it may, that is, no matter how the pigs arrived on the island, the fact is that they are there and, indeed, they know how to swim. And it is true that these cute little animals attract tourists. They are calm, you can feed them, touch them, take pictures with them ... Whatever you want.

And this "Whatever you want" is what has misled many tourists who, like good humans, think that "Whatever you want" is that you can mistreat them, get them drunk, give them sand mixed with food, steal their babies to take selfies ... All this human affection has led to the death of several pigs (as now it can lead to error, I will specify that they are the pigs living on the island, not the tourist pigs) due to indigestion, stress and other conditions.

But not only that, also the pigs (inhabitants of the island) have been involved in lawsuits against the pigs (tourists). Yes, that's right, and in most cases, the two-legged have made a common front and have won, condemning to death (sacrifice, they call it) those with four for having bitten a vacationer who had borrowed only one a moment to her baby. The mother, father or legal guardian of the suckling baby, wrapped in a mixture of

46

anger and fear, had jumped against the invader giving him as a Souvenir of Big Major (Made in China) a beautiful scar in the shape of pig teeth. After the gratuitous attack (?) The human biped decided to report it to some biped policemen and they came to a biped judge who ruled that the quadruped pig, as punishment for biting defending his quadruped son, should die.

Justice they call it.

THE ISLAND OF THE CATS

At first it was the old men of the place, then it was the books and now it is the internet that has the accumulated wisdom of eons of knowledge. Yes, I know, it is a too simple reduction and an exaggeration at the same time, but I liked the phrase and I decided to leave it at that. Well, since we can find everything on the Internet and most people believe everything they read without knowing if any semi-literate has written it with a computer and a wifi stolen from a coffee shop, I'll tell you that one day I found a t-shirt that read " I was normal before the third cat ".

We all have (at least those of my generation) the image of the Crazy Cat from The Simpsons throwing felines at whoever dared to disturb her. If you are from another generation or just those yellow beings gave you a little creep or their jokes did not make you laugh, surely in your neighborhood you will find your particular Crazy of the Cats (there are also some men, but generally they are women. Men are more likely to feed the pigeons above their bellies while they sit comfortably in the sun on a park bench or plaza. Fun fact: they generally have small feet.).

I have never understood the passion for cats, but that is another topic, please come back.

Well, Aoshima would be the paradise of the fans of the felines or, who knows, if a higher step than they could not bear to reach. A much higher step. And it is that this island, Aoshima, goes quite a few steps further: statistics say that it has 15 human inhabitants and more than 100 cats. They would touch more than seven per beard, but surely there is someone who does not like them, which adds up to the average. I know, it is not the only Island of the Cats in Japan, but it is one of the most famous, and in this chapter we launch into the commercial.

PUT A CAT IN YOUR LIFE

Aoshima is a small island of fishermen located in the Ehime prefecture, in Japan. At the end of World War II, the population reached 900 inhabitants, but as has happened in many corners of the globe with the industrialization of society, young people do not want hard jobs in the fields or the sea and prefer a stable profession (¿I said stable? Sorry...) and little by little they left. Depopulation, they call it. So there were only a few elderly people left on the island who refused from what had been their home for their entire lives. So far, the history of any people in any country. But friend, now comes the good.

In its time, the coasts of the island were infested with merchant ships that, either by call or by destination, docked in its ports. That, at the end of the Great War, was also in the past, but we are interested in that time to understand what is now. So let's start again.

Merchant ships arriving on the island, when were still approaching the island, had cats on board. Not because they liked them, the captain was one of the few Crazy Cats in the world or they used them as lookouts because of their ease of climbing the mast. No, cats were used to kill the rat plagues that often infested their ships. But we all know about the relationship between cats and water, so we can imagine that life on these ships would not be the most satisfactory for cats, who would be wanting to touch dry land and kiss the sand that took them away from the aquatic element. So more than one, disgusted by life at sea, decided to discreetly defect, whistling down the ramp, and stay and live in the first port that was somewhat lax with visa-free immigrants. Aoshima was the destiny of many of them. Who knows if there was a knock-on effect, a family reunification or it was a mere chance, but there they founded their new colony proclaiming, as the Europeans did in America, "I have discovered this land and now it belongs to me."

Thus, cats were accumulating on the island and humans disappearing, emigrating towards uncertain but more tempting futures, or dying just like merchant ships and fishing boats. The only bipedal inhabitants left were those who no longer worked due to their advanced age and, to hang out and have company, they dedicated their time to caring for and feeding moustache and all their offspring.

WHERE IS THE MARQUETIN PLAN?

Currently, the ships are coming back to the island. But they are not merchant ships, well, maybe they are, but they do not carry goods to the spindle, but people. A ferry arrives at Aoshima twice a day, which can hold 34 people. That's it. I mean that the island has become a tourist attraction in the area, but there is no other service: there are no restaurants, no hotels, no souvenir shops, or vending machines ... Nothing. You go, you see the cats and you come back. And this, in the times in which we live, is the great news that should amaze us all. Aoshima needs a good farm plan to take advantage of the cats, and the money to the thousands of travelers who land each year. Cat lovers who would surely like to carry a stuffed pussycat, eat a BigCat hamburguer or buy a bag of feed (diet) to offer to cats as if they were ducks in a pond.

A PROBLEM OF OBESITY

Yes, I just said I think in diet and it is for a compelling reason (sorry for the easy joke). Cats, between the food they search for on their own, that which the human inhabitants of the island give them and that which they receive from tourists, are immersed in a curve towards obesity that is beginning to worry experts. In addition, the exercise that cats do is scarce, since they do not hunt because, basically, they do not need it and also because they have finished with all the pests of the island that could interest them.

Sedentary lifestyle, excess food, contemplative life... I think I am beginning to understand the reasons that unite us with cats.

3.
WHEN YOU THINK HE'S AN ARCHITECT AND HE ACTUALLY IS AN ARTIST

THE REVERSE IS GOING BACK

Agatha Chistie wrote a book called *The Crooked House*. The Tower of Pisa is crooked. Even the floors of many houses where you leave a ball and it starts to roll are also crooked. But what I'm going to tell you now is far beyond a slight incline. It is as if in Photoshop you had said "and what happens if I put Rotate 180º?".

They say that popular culture is very wise and rarely wrong. And when I speak of popular culture I mean that knowledge transmitted from generation to generation that gives us life lessons in tweets format from before cybernetic social networks were invented, that is, in sayings loaded with common sense, observation and/or ancestral science.

There are economic, meteorological, behavioral, loving, gastronomic... In fact, we almost have a saying for every occasion. Even some that contradict each other so that you can choose the one that most appeals to you or interests you at a certain time. Some are cryptic, others more understandable. Some make a lot of sense, others have already lost their strength. There are those who do not know for sure if they are right, and those who do not involve any doubt, such as that the house cannot be started from the roof... Or is it possible?

BREAKING MYTHS

Well, it seems that you can, you just have to turn the house and turn it upside down. And this is it, as easy and as simple as turning it around. And this is what many owners have done trying to make their houses as original as possible. Oh the originality... Like when a music group thought that playing their songs with a ukulele would be original until they realized that they were in the fashion of making music with that pygmy guitar. The problem with being original when you are not the first (or the only one) is that in the end they end up doing it so many that you stop (or almost stop) being original.

And it is that the globe is full of houses that have their roof embedded in the earth and the foundations are like branches dancing in the west wind one spring morning. Well, maybe plagued is not the most suitable word ... It is not that you find in every neighborhood a house upside down or, when you see an empty lot, you think about whether they are going to build it up or down. No, it is not so normal, but it is more than one might expect or imagine. Some examples? The WonderWorks in Orlando, Florida; Myrtle Beach, in South Carolina; the Haus steht Kopf, in Tyrol, Austria; the Upside Down House, in Niagara Falls; Die Welt steht Kopf, in Trassenheide, on the island of Usedom, Germany; or the Upside Down House, in Szymbark, Poland. All of them have been built starting with the roof.

LIVING THERE IS IMPOSSIBLE

Upside down houses have a small drawback that makes their sale not so easy, even if the prices of the houses were reasonable and people like you and me could buy them without having to mortgage us 90 years after having sold a kidney and half liver on the black market to pay the entrance.

These types of houses not only have their external appearance upside down, they also have the interior. When you enter you walk on the ceilings and all the furniture is anchored to the ground, that is, above our heads: sofas, beds, tables, chairs, even the cars parked in the garage are mysteriously violating the forces of gravity. It is as if the house were built and inhabited in a conventional way but a tornado or a green giant decided to turn them over after gluing all the elements so that they would not come loose. Even window shades are cleverly fastened so they don't lose their natural drape... upwards, in this case!

For all this, and as you can imagine, houses upside down are not habitable. They are generally tourist attractions and are located in theme parks or in areas with a large number of people. Of course, where they are, they always triumph, since queues to enter are common. Who has never wanted to walk on the roof of their house?

And don't tell me that yours is upside down because you have it upside down, that's another problem and another saying. But don't worry, I have children, I know what you're talking about.

REFRAIN SHY PEOPLE

You leave the house that it is still night. You work eight or ten hours surrounded by people. You eat at menu restaurants packed with strangers. In the subway they touch you in places that you did not know had tact. People in the supermarket queue have no notion of what living space means. Someone you do not know calls you and asks your name and tells you what you need, even if you repeat that you are not interested, because they know very well what is good for you. On the street you dodge mobile phones that don't watch where they are going and an electric scooter steps on your foot without flinching. People, noise, stress ... But finally you get home, you close the door and the outside world is far away, you are at peace.

Unless you live in a completely transparent glass house! As you say? It can not be? That does not exist? Don't be naive, if you've read this far you know that human imagination (and stupidity) can reach unsuspected levels. Ask again.

Exists?

Well yes, there is. And I love that you ask me this spontaneous question because I wanted to talk to you about it. Of course, it is in Japan, in Tokyo more specifically, and not in the suburbs, but in a residential neighborhood. It is the work of the architect Sou Fujimoto and is made entirely of glass with a metal skeleton.

I have made this point and aside so that you would have a few moments to reflect on the subject. I suppose that in this age when we post everything on social networks, we have reached a point where privacy is much less valued than a few years ago, but the passage from cyberspace to physical space is a bit uncomfortable for me. It is one thing to hang what I want, even if it is the most ridiculous or the most intimate, and another is that anyone who passes by the street or my own neighbors can look inside my house as visitors to a neighborhood zoo.

Only the peanut machine is missing at the entrance.

THE CONCEPT OF A TREE ESCAPES ME
According to Sou Fujimoto, he devised this project as a tree. The twenty-one rooms that make up the

house are conceived as if they were branches: all of them interconnected on several floors and each with a different function. This is how the architect describes it, who took two years to design it and carried out 11 different projects before he could break the residential space with the glass tree.

Perhaps the wood with which the furniture that decorates the interior is made helps this feeling of living in a tree, but the similarity escapes me. And even if this were the case, did it occur to anyone during all the time they took to think about the project that we stopped living in the trees for something? Privacy, security, warm...

Be that as it may, this is the inspiration that Fujimoto explains to describe his project, although I think that depending on the time you look at the house, it will look more like an 85 m2 showcase of the Red Light District in Amsterdam than a simple family home in Tokyo. I guess you understand what I mean ...

WITH WHAT IT COST TO CLEAN THE WINDOWS
And we come to the last point that I suppose has not escaped you, not even because of the title of this section. Right! How do we clean all of this? Because if we find it difficult to clean the windows of an ordinary house or the windows of our stores and premises, imagine cleaning all the walls and not having a single one of those damn wet lines that always escape us and that we do not see until It has become dry and to remove it

63

we must clean all the glass again (at least, on one side). It reminds me a bit of the woman who had the Guinness Record for the longest hair in the world and who took a whole day to wash it.

RAISE THE CURTAIN

EMPLOYEE
Mr boss, the next two days I won't be able to come to work.

BOSS
Sorry? I don't think I understand you.

EMPLOYEE
I have to make the crystals at home.

BOSS
Where do you live? In a giant fish tank?

EMPLOYEE
More or less...

LOWER THE CURTAIN

The good thing is that it takes away many other headaches: you do not have to think about which paintings you will hang (or they would have to be painted on both sides), what will be the dining room color or if the stem you expect will be a boy or a girl to choose between blue or pink (I know, this is archaic, but it is an easy example), it will all depend on the color of the facade of the opposite building.

DO NOT GET FAT, NOT EVEN A GRAM

I had a classmate who just talking about syringes and needles would turn white, get dizzy and fall collapsed on the floor. No kidding, I saw it. There are also those who go up to an elevator and get cold sweats, pounding heartbeats and a small (or large) hyperventilation works its way from their lungs through the windpipe. If you are one of these, that is, the claustrophobic, this house is not for you. But if you are one of the very claustrophobic, like my classmate who only heard about the subject, you notice that your head leaves the place where it usually is, stop reading and skip to the next chapter.

A NARROW VISION

It all started in 2012 with a coffee, a walk and a vision. The artist and architect Jakub Szczęsny was walking quietly through Warsaw (Poland) when he saw that, between two blocks of flats, a new one and an old one, there was a space of little more than a meter but that it was neither a street nor a passage. It was just a dead, empty space, nothingness. And that nothing inspired him to make the narrowest house in the world.

It is located between 22 Chłodna Street and 74 Żelazna Street and is called La Casa Keret, since its owner is the Israeli writer Etgar Keret, who says that it is an ideal place to write since it avoids distractions. He also explains that it is a tribute to his parents, who were locked up in Nazi camps during World War II. Not only because of the claustrophobic space, but because, a few meters away, there was a wooden bridge that connected the Long Ghetto with the Warsaw one.

FOR POLAND, IT IS NOT A HOUSE
When IKEA came into our lives (yes, my young reader, the Swedish giant of cardboard-stuffed furniture has not always been with us) and with IKEA also came those models of floors in which they claim that you can live with everything. which has a 60 m2 house, most of us put our hands on our heads and prayed that we would have a space to hide in when we argue with the couple. Well, that was because we didn't know the Keret house. Polish, however, have not institutionalized the dimensions of this narrow house to design future Ideal Couples apartments.

Under Polish law, the building does not meet the minimum requirements to be considered a dwelling, so it is listed as an art installation. And it is that it measures 1.5 meters in its widest part, and does not reach the meter in its narrowest part, adding a total of 14.5 m2. With these measures we might think that there is no space for minimum services, but it is not like that: there is a shower, sink, kitchen, bed, desk... Everything that a house should have, only that one thing is closer to the other and to a somewhat smaller size. And to get from one place to another, sometimes, specially located stairs must be used.

Built with a metal frame and with its opaque glass façade, Jakub Szczęsny says it is the most complicated project he has ever faced in his life. For example, another curious thing is that, to make the most of the space, you enter through the ground, that is to say, that the door, when closed, is part of the parquet on which you walk on the ground floor.

I hope that the heirs of Mr. IKEA never read this book, I would not want to be the seed of, economically, fruitful ideas for builders and pseudo-cabinet makers on an industrial scale.

TO VISIT OR SPEND THE NIGHT
The Keret House is open to the public on some days, but tickets sell out quickly, so it's best to check availability before trying to enter. In 10 minutes you have the visit done (there is not much to see either) and a maximum of 4 people can enter per shift.

But there are those who are luckier and are allowed to spend a night there. They are generally artists and writers that Keret allows to enjoy the experience, who knows if to escape the real world and worldly distractions and focus on their works, or perhaps they are moved by simple curiosity (as most of us) but they are lucky to meet the right person.

One way or another, it would not be the house of our dreams to spend a quarantine or a zombie apocalypse. Although well thought out, to protect the fort you would not need 300 Spartans: Thermopylae would be a waste of space.

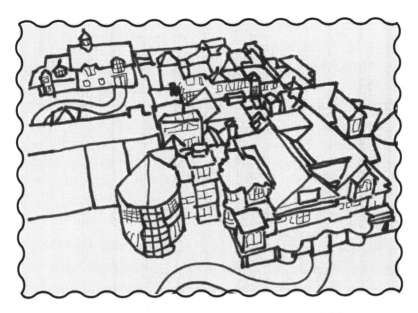

THE RIFLES THAT FORGED A HOUSE

I'll start with the facts as we know them: a billionaire widow who had also lost her only son; a sense of guilt that leaves Mulder, by comparison, at the height of a Trap Producer; more money than The Chichos spent (presumably) on drugs in the 1970s; more workers than in the happy hour of sun and shade in a bar with a Coca-Cola sign; and a half-left house in California. Thus began the history of Winchester Manor.

THE BRICK IS ALWAYS THE SOLUTION

Sara Winchester inherited a lump of money and also an income that today would be equivalent to about 26,000 euros a day, euro above euro below, which I don't want to get my fingers caught. That fortune was fattened by the sale of the repeating shotguns that forged

America, killing people by the handful. And of course, that worried Sara. A medium seems to have recommended the ancestral remedy for this type of case: since time immemorial, the internal problems of the rich and powerful families of the world have been solved with labyrinths.

If we look at the myth, the first situation in which the troubles of a family ended in the construction of a vast labyrinth was in ancient Greece, specifically on the island of Crete. The queen fell in love with the palace bull, things that happen, and Daedalus, father of all inventors from Da Vinci to your school science teacher, saw reef and first built the disease, a mechanical cow with capacity for a queen in supine position, and then the remedy: a labyrinth where to hide a minotaur. Wow, like any pharmaceutical company. The thing became more and more Greek and ended up in rescue and brothers killing brothers, or at least half brothers.

Sara Winchester decided to lock her mental ghosts in a kitsch maze painted red, with a mixture of varied architectural styles, rococo decoration of new rich, stairs that lead nowhere, windows to other rooms, secret passages, peepholes, an obsession with the number thirteen, just two mirrors and a bathroom and who knows what. There was no architect or plan. It was a do it yourself but with a hundred workers throwing compliments.

THE THEORIES WE LIKE SO MUCH
There are two theories to understand why Sara tried to give Le Corbusier an aneurysm. One says that Sara

wanted to hide from vengeful ghosts, specifically those killed by her husband's weapons. It is the one that has triumphed at the horror movie level. The other says that the house was built to comfortably house the host of ghosts. That is the one I like. Because, after all, leaving aside its non-Euclidean constructive logic, the house is very welcoming.

In fact, it is more than cozy. It is a great-aunt's wet dream: there is no piece of furniture that does not weigh two tons and has up to fourteen moldings and reliefs, the beds are canopied, there are thousands of curtains gracefully gathered with twine and pompoms, Persian rugs, chandeliers, Tiffany stained glass and dark wood walls. The thing is deeply recharged.

It is not a house to hide from the dead, it seems that Sara wants to entertain them. In the extreme and unhealthy way in which the great-aunt that I mentioned before would do it, but translating the food into architecture. Imagine how happy the ghosts roam that house, sheltering thousands. Benevolent and lost idle beams of light that wander in eternal loops through Sara Winchester's amiable labyrinth.

A MORE EARTHLY THEORY

There is a third possibility that some historians suggest: that everything is a fat woman's lie. We'll see. As noted, Sara Winchester was a real nice lady, who had a regular crew of workers on staff, bought them houses and left them money in her will. The proof: the daughters of almost all of Sara's workers were named Sara. In addition, most of the strange things about the house are due to the lack of plan and the clumsy arrangements

made after the 1906 earthquake that almost devasta-
ted it. Before 1906 the house was huge and very tall,
afterwards, if it grew, it grew wide. It appears that the
repairs were made in a hurry. Stairs that lead nowhere
used to lead to parts that are gone. Furthermore, Sara
did not seem to believe in mediums more than the rest
of her contemporaries, that they were incredibly gulli-
ble. Furthermore, the profusion of thirteen-element series seems, by all accounts, a later addition.

FROM HOME TO FAIR ATTRACTION
Ultimately, Sara Winchester created a monument to
excess, a cultivation of architecture in the Petri dish of
the world. An ugly and brilliant wonder. It was impossible that all this did not pay homage to the most twisted
of fantasies.

Five months after Sara's death, a family of former
showmen, specialists in carnivals and monster and
wonder shows, turned the mansion into a tourist attraction. Between its labyrinth the myth of the cursed
house was woven. That is the great history of the world:
chance and contingency turned into meaning and legend.

The house survived fires, earthquakes, large depres-
sions, and the Devil's general condemnation of California. It is one of the most visited places in the entire
state. It makes sense: tourists and ghosts have always
gotten along, the two exist in strange loops, life-like si-
mulations.

4.
DREAM HOTELS
(OR NIGHTMARE)

A BEER HELPS YOU SLEEP

Vermouth time. That hour that should be imposed by law but that, ordinary people, we can only enjoy a few days a year. Those olives, those *bravas*, those pickled anchovies, those cockles... Nothing better than a good vermouth that connects with food and lasts until nap time.

And to wash it all down and make the doughy mass of the frozen and reheated potato chips go better to our famished stomach, nothing better than a cold beer to withstand the heat of July on the terrace of the main bar. But this ancient brew also carries risks! And it is not because of the alcohol, which is also because of the hops, a plant from the same family as cannabis...

Who hasn't gotten that pleasant and irresistible drowsiness after a few beers? Something that would leave you asleep on the sofa without much consideration or, even, on the table of the bar where you are tasting the canned delicacies of world gastronomy, with the sun and the children playing in the distance ... Oh, who could have a bed at those times! But what if the solution, the bed, was in the can?

THE HOTEL FOR VERY BREWERS
Well yes, a bed inside the beer can. Okay, you're more like a barrel or bottle, but let's say that the bar you're in is one of those places that are on the corner, with bison cigarettes in the ashtray, paper napkins, the kind that don't clean, wrinkled and lying between the bar and lame stools, and a waiter who you pester every time you order something. Yes? Now do you see that you have been served canned beer? Well then, let's start again.

Well yes, a bed inside the beer can. No, you are not dreaming or the alcohol has gone to my head. Nor have I invented a miniaturizer that allows you to take your mattress and put it inside the aluminum, I am talking about the Hotel Can Sleep, in Denmark.

Located near the lake Skandeborg (in the center-east of the Danish peninsula) is one of the most unique hotels, not to mention rare, in the world. In the middle of a meadow in a paradisiacal environment, there are

3.80-meter-high cans grouped in 20 packs of 6 plus the occasional loose can that make up the 121 rooms of Hotel Can Sleep.

TWO-PLANT CANS

Each can-room has 2 floors: in the first, of course, there is a bar cabinet full of Royal Unibrez beers, and the rooms are faithful replicas of the cans of this popular Danish beer. I do not know if the brand in question is a sponsor or investor of this peculiar hotel, but common sense tells us that they should not be outside the project.

The second floor is accessed via stairs. In it we find a round bed for two people. This is the standard rating for each of the rooms, although they can host up to three guests. Of course, you have to notify in advance so that they put something similar to an auxiliary bed.

The upper part of the can, that is, what would be the ceiling, is a large glass skylight that allows you to see the sky and be able to sleep under the stars. Although depending on the beers you have had on the lower floor, perhaps what is best for you is to sleep on your stomach, more than anything as a precaution. But since you get to sleep one night in the Can Sleep, you better enjoy all the pleasures in moderation, since it is not easy to get a room.

WITH THE INTENTION IS NOT ENOUGH, YOU NEED LUCK

Yes, I know, right now you are about to put down your book to ask Mr. Google how much it costs to sleep in this hotel to book your next vacation, but the shape of the rooms is not the only surprise that Can Sleep entails: The hotel is only open during the month of August (coinciding with the celebration of the Danish music festival Smukfest) and there are so many requests for accommodation that they receive, that they are awarded by lottery among all reservations.

But if it's your turn, you go preparing the portfolio, since the price per night is about 500 euros. Of course, how many people can say that they have slept inside a beer can?

A VERY COMFORTABLE COLON

—Where are you going for holidays this year?
—The back arse of nowhere!

Sorry for the obscenity and the easy joke, but the subject is worth it. And it is that to whom it occurs to make a hotel with the shape of a colon? Yes, I was not wrong with accents and capital letters. I am not referring to Colón (Christopher Columbus in Spain), I am referring to the colon, the final part of the digestive system. Well, someone came up with it and it materialized as the Hotel Casanus.

I know, a lot of questions come to mind. I'll try to answer some of them before you ask them:

"Yes, the anus is also visible."
"No, it's not the front door."
"Yes, I also consider it a great failure."

I HAVE NOT UNDERSTOOD ART FOR A LONG TIME

This hotel, rather this hotel room since it consists of a single room ...

SECTION: I don't know if the idea was to do the entire digestive system and set up a large complex, but they ran out of budget. If so, Messrs. Gates, Ortega, Bezos, Zuckerberg ... seriously consider a small investment that this promises. END OF SECTION

Well, the Hotel Casanus is located in Stekene, in Belgium, near Antwerp. I thought of Belgians as serious people who drew Tintin, made beer, ate mussels, and planted cabbages. But it seems that no, it is seen that they were dazzled by the Dutch artist and sculptor Joep Van Lieshout and they let him plant his huge butt in the Verbeke Foundation Sculpture Park (sorry for another easy joke).

WHAT IS A COLON LIKE?

Think of the majestic hotels set in castles and imperial buildings. Or in the small charming hotels. You got it? Yes? Well now erase it,the Hotel Casanus has nothing to do with them. Nor with those of the big chains: impersonal photocopies of their predecessors. Nor with the dilapidated pensions in the old quarters of tourist cities. No dude, I'm talking about a human colon! To be honest, this is the first that I see live and direct, and I hope it is the last, since, objectively, it is not something beautiful to look at.

This hotel room is elongated and curved like a worm, red as the entrails and with some marked in swollen veins decorating its entire surface. Wow, the house we've all wanted to be built on the land next to our house to enhance the views of a decaying organic matter dump and seagulls fighting for every piece of food with rats big as wild boars. But hey, this is just the outside. Let's go in.

Once inside (I have already told you the mistake, in my opinion, made with the entrance), a non-existent decoration leaves space for comfortable double beds, a full bathroom and a great heating so that your ... (no, I won't say, but you know what I was going for). Nothing else. Diaphanous, some would say. Scarce in details like a Seat Panda, others would say. Unfinished, I would say. But, in short, it remains, again, just my humble opinion.

IF THE WORM BITES YOU...
(OK, I'LL STOP WITH THE EASY JOKES)
Agree. I know. You're right. Perhaps I have laughed too much at this hotel, and more so when you find out that the reservations to spend the night in it are constant and it is worth more than 120 euros a stay.

Travelers of all stripes are drawn to the Casanus, but some of the top customers are modern art amateurs who can't wait to stay in Joep Van Lieshout's colon (couldn't help it).

Oh yes, it has paradisiacal surroundings, with a lake, swans and the starry sky of a summer night. There is no better place to plant your ass.

A ROOM FOR EVERY DARK FANTASY

In our dreams, in our most hidden mind from society, each one of us hides his own Mr. Hyde. That monster that we think that if we bring to light we will be left without family, without a partner and without friends. We even find ourselves locked in a small jail with the lewd and unrecognized older brother of a certain Hightower who was out at Crazy Police Academy. But in reality, almost all of us (and I would like to emphasize the almost in this sentence) would feel more liberated and could share those dark corners with the darkness of others. If we bring them to light, would they stop being dark?

Well, there is a place where we can live a little of our most intimate fantasies, at least at bedtime (and whatever arises). Would you rather sleep in a coffin, in a cell, in a dungeon, in a room with the bed on the ceiling, in a kaleidoscope...? These are some of the rooms that are proposed to you at the Propeller Island Hotel, in Berlin (Germany).

GREATNESS IS BORN FROM NEED

The idea came from the twisted and needy mind of an artist named Lars Strorschen. At the end of 1997, December to be more exact: the boy was a bit short of cash and decided to rent some rooms in his apartment, to reach the end of the month and pay the bills... which we have all done. But I think (and it is pure personal speculation) how fair it should not be if before renting them he thoroughly renovated them so that they had something different: the symbol room, the orange room, the castle room and the mirror room. He baptized all of this with the name of the Jules Verne novel, Propeller Island Hotel. Given the success he was having, he was buying different flats that were sold on the farm (I said, that it was not very fair).

At this point, let's make a reflection: I suppose that the more floors it had, the more people who liked to sleep in coffins would walk around the block ... It would be logical to think that the neighbors of all life did not take long to sell and at a good price , also.

In 2013 it already had 30 rooms, which are more rare, and today it has 45, the reception, an art gallery and a breakfast room set as if it were a tropical garden. You can sleep in flying beds, in sarcophagi, in cages ... The catalog is extensive and for (almost) all tastes. It is also possible that what you are looking for is a room with two beds, a night table and a sink. If so, you have the wrong chapter. In fact, I think you even got the wrong book. Even so, if you want to know a little more about this hotel, read on.

LET'S TALK ABOUT PRICES

The price of the Propeller Island Hotel ... Well, it is not at all unreasonable, but I would not say that it is an establishment to spend many nights in it. And not because of the price, but because nightmares can abound when you return to the seclusion of your home. The cost of the room ranges between 70 and 180 euros per night, depending on the type of decoration you choose (we all know how expensive coffins are).

You can add additional guests to the reservation, but each additional person, with a maximum of three, pays an extra 15 euros. There is also the option to change rooms. Some reasons could be because you do not like it, because you prefer another or because that night you have not managed to sleep due to fear or discomfort. If so, you can move under payment of a supplement of 25 euros. That taking into account that there is availability.

When art and restoration come together, a lot can come out. Some of them even exceptional, but generally they tend to be rare, expensive and curious things, more than beautiful. Here, for example, an unforgettable experience was born. Would you spend a dream night? Personally I would not assure you. But I guess, if you go, it's not for sleeping all night long. Some torture at twelve, in the cage from one to two, your image multiplied by a thousand for a while longer, a funeral at four... The normal thing in any hotel.

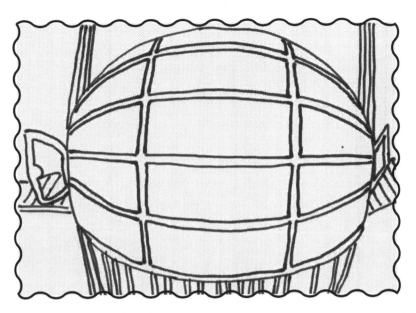

LOOK FOR ANOTHER THING IF YOU HAVE VERTIGO

If you've seen the Game of Thrones series, this hotel would be the closest thing to the cell where Tyrion Lannister is put in the Eagles' Nest. Right, the one that only has three walls and, in the absence of the fourth, a free fall of half Everest. And yes, I have vertigo and those scenes still wake me up between screaming and sweating some nights, you can't imagine how bad I had it watching those episodes.

Well, this hotel would be the same only with crystals and without sadistic jailers who enjoy beating and humiliating you with a club and throwing the little food they give you to the ground. Wow, all the fun is gone. It's like a wish and they don't let me be a creative medieval torture room because, from my humble point of view,

they have made these small but significant changes because there are very picky people who demand little
of you and close the joint. Although to see who goes up
there to check if you have open or the doors are still
with the judicial seal. Don't you know which hotel I'm
talking about? Step by step, my young Padawan.

HEIGHT ROOMS

Now seriously, I'm talking about the Skylodge Adventure Suites, in Peru. Three methacrylate balls sus-
pended in the vertical stone wall 400 meters from the
ground with views of the Sacred Valley of the Incas, one
hour from the city of Cusco. The creative company, Na-
tura Vive, calls them Vertical Housing Modules (VHM)
and they measure 7.5 meters long by 2.6 meters high.
There is no running water in them, so there is no shower
and the bathroom is what they call a dry bath. There are
some barrels so you can hydrate, but the bottle must be
brought by you. What they do have is light, and I don't
mean natural light, which too (they must be the brigh-
test hotel rooms in the world), but lamps powered by
solar energy.

And if you want less daylight, there are curtains. It is
also in case you want to have a little privacy. Who can
see you 400 meters from the ground? Well, some win-
ged neighbors called condors who live in those parts.
Although if you go up there and pay what it's worth to
sleep, it would not be very sensible to draw the curtains,
but it is again just my humble opinion. Don't you know
how to climb? But it is the best! Well, I save it for last.

Of the three balls, sorry, Vertical Housing Modules, only two are rooms (Silves and Miranda), the other, Luna, is intended for services. And it is that beyond sleeping, full board is also offered. The Skylodge has space to sleep twelve people, with beds, pillows, down duvets, sheets ... I do not know if every morning they take it out the window and air everything, to the next guest, but take the clothes to the Laundry must be quite an adventure.

Of course, if you want to sleep in a good hotel and this only serves to upload photos to your Instagram, then you can choose the option of using the suite as a dining room: you go up, eat and come back down. The concept of lunch with a view never made so much sense. Oh, and (humble and also very subjective opinion), they dangerously serve alcoholic beverages.

GETTING THERE IS NOT EASY

I have decided that I will tell you before the end, but just a little before, that let's see if you get used to it and think that they are going to give you everything for your pretty face.

How do we get to the Vertical Housing Modules? Well, whoever imagines an elevator to go up to the room, should be looking for another accommodation. There are only two ways to get there: through the via ferrata or the network of zip lines that range from 150 to 700 meters in length. If you have ever climbed a mountain, you will know what tires you and what you sweat ... Let's look back, you remember that I mentioned that

91

there are no showers, right? Well that. Luckily, the hotel information specifies that there are six windows and four vents... They must be very necessary for an overnight stay!

When we want to go down, we must do the reverse route. Yes, I think I have also commented about alcoholic beverages, zip lines and via ferratas ... Perhaps now you are of the same opinion as me and you also say "dangerously they serve alcoholic beverages", but I don't want to influence your reasoning too much.

ORDER IN ADVANCE

CLIENT
Nothing, I was over here and I wondered if you had a room ...

RECEPTION
Let me see... No, I have everything packed tonight. But tomorrow I have one free. Do you want me to keep it for you?

CLIENT
No, if I make up my mind, I'll come back to see if there's any luck.

RECEPTION
As you prefer. Have a happy descent.

END

This is a conversation that never happens at this hotel. The trips are organized in advance with pick up and return to the city of Cusco by the staff. The price?

About 500 euros per person and night; and about 250 euros to go up and have lunch there (travel and equipment included).

Let me give one last humble and personal opinion: I go from paying to be suffering all night in case the balls, okay, Vertical Housing Modules, fall, thinking that the next day I have to go down and pay 500 euros on top. That's counting that I make it to the top alive. Yes, vertigo is screwed up. But it's your decision... There are people for everything in the Lord's vineyard!

So now you know, if vertigo does not suit you and Game of Thrones did not traumatize you, here is a destiny that will make you stop talking about the same old battles at dinners with your friends. But be careful not to repeat yourself too much with the "I slept with the condors", which from the fifth time seems heavy.

THEMED BUSES

Living in abandoned buses. The concept is reminiscent of dystopian future movies like Mad Max, with neck chains, tight leather, muzzles and flamethrowers. Are you interested in a hotel like this? Well, I'm sorry, if it exists, I don't know it. No, nothing could be further from the reality I want to talk about. Actually, take Mad Max, look for the opposite extreme, go a little further and you'll be getting closer to the concept of this hotel. Yes, yes, I'm still talking about abandoned buses.

The gossips say that some horror movie scripts have been written here (sorry for the poetic license I have taken, but I have not found any data that says otherwise, so like the Yeti: somebody show me that it is not! true!).

We continue with the references, in this case, more than cinephiles, television. The Paw Patrol. Those of you who have small children, or have lived with one since 2013, will unfortunately know what I'm talking about.

(AUTHOR'S NOTE, that is, mine: I am writing in 2020, the year of global confinement. If this book has survived the passage of time and you are reading these lines in, for example, 2055, I hope this reference no longer sounds familiar to you Please don't let it sound like you. It wouldn't make much sense for you to read the book if it wasn't for an archaeological or nostalgic theme. END OF THE NOTE)

Well, if you know the (infamous) Paw Patrol, remember what Rocky says: "Before throwing it away, recycle it." And this is precisely what they have done in the Chinese Tai Tai Mountain Park, in Taiyuan, Shanxi province, since 2016: they have remodeled buses that were already out of circulation and turned them into hotel rooms.

A CURIOUS DECOR, LET'S LEAVE IT THERE

One next to the other, as if it were a parking of heavy machines. This is how they have designed this field that houses more than 30 thematically decorated buses both inside and out. And you may be wondering, decorated with what? Let's go to the mess!

Mikey Mouse, Hello Kitty! o Doraemon are some of the characters that inspire each of the rooms in which we can stay. The exterior painting with drawings of the characters; the interior tinted with its corporate colors (pink for Kitty, blue for Doraemon...); stuffed animals, cups, sheets, cushions...

Each room has all the details to make us get fed up with our favorite character if the holidays are too long, that is, more than a day. If we have taken the last one that was left and we do not like the theme, we may end up sleeping in the open.

PRICE AND PERFORMANCE RATIO

As always, the big question surrounding this hotel, and many others, is where do people get these wicked ideas? I believe that substances that take you to alternative realities may have something to do with it, but I prefer not to get into a mess that I won't know how to get out of without a trial and a well-deserved fine.

They say the idea came from seeing the number of disused buses in the market, buried in rubble, in sheds or rusting in any field lost from the hand of God. The idea gave way to the budget; and the budget to a business that could be profitable.

The promoters say that buying and adapting one of these vehicles in apartments with bathroom, kitchen, bed, furniture... costs around 9,000 euros. If you have done reforms at home, you know that this figure comes out only by remodeling the dining room, so yes, it is economically interesting. But if you also think that the interior space of a bus exceeds 20 m2, you realize that it is very similar to an IKEA house. And the price for sleeping there is not excessive either, given the eccentricities that exist in the world: between 40 and 50 euros a night.

Of course, going out for a twilight walk is like doing it in the summer camp or when you come back from dinner and you don't know exactly where you have parked your car in the open. But when you come in ... Oh when you come in! The monochrome paradise you have chosen is waiting for you. You close the door and enjoy.

Nightmares are not included in the price.

5.
HALF WITH NATURE

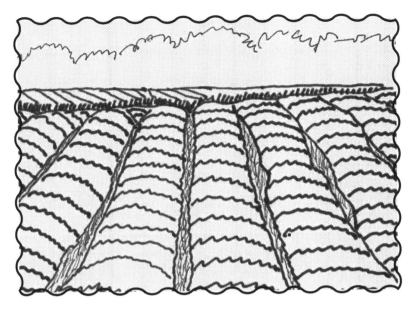

YOUR VIOLET DAY

Imagine you are driving on a fifteenth-level French highway and the only thing your eyes can see through your sunburned retinas are fields of lavender. Thousands of meters and meters. Plots, farms, extensions and large landed estates dedicated exclusively to growing purple flowers.

You are in Valensole, but you could also be somewhere else in French Provence, the kingdom of lavender. If you roll down the window, you will smell its intense aroma and die of intense heat: imagine that you are in the middle of the worst August that has desolated Christianity. It is the flowery season. We are already located, let's go for its inhabitants.

Who lives here? I wonder. And you should also ask yourself. After all, we are talking about a whole region dedicated to lavender monoculture.

VAMPIRES OF WHAT?

Are they vegan vampires who have replaced flowers for blood? Are vegan dandy vampires who live by smelling flowers? Are vampires dandies vegan yogis that for living only need to contemplate flowers and touch the strange tube that gives you a headache?

The answer has to do with the global economy: they are vampires, that is clear, but they live off the blood, sweat and certain extravagant cultural mechanisms of Chinese tourists. Well, and that the kilo of lavender is paid one hundred and seventeen euros (price of 2019), which is not bad.

Traffic slows down as you get closer to the heart of the lavender fields. The Venusian landscape that surrounds you, intensified by that optical effect of the sun roasting the earth, never seems to have been stepped on by man, woman or any other dog.

And I ask again, who lives here? Lava beings who rush their short lives between birth and solidification?

THE ENIGMATIC TRAFFIC SIGNS

There is a huge, blue sign a few meters away. It shows a car in foreshortening and fields in perspective, everything with the typical schematics of traffic signs, whose only realistic figure appear to be the jumping elk and the still cow (this time there is neither). On the drawn fields, a series of human figures appear that seem to carry out a particular type of dance. Maybe they are afflicted by the San Vito's disease or some type of demonic possession. There is another figure on the poster, the one of a little man at a traffic light who seems to be taking photos of the crazy dancers.

What must happen? It is clear that this is one of those territories in the world where you and your couple can be ritually murdered by the locals before or after they burn your bodies inside a wicker man. Your daughters will be raised in a pantheistic and atavistic community and will grow up to be witches or Waldorf free school teachers.

Are the jumping dolls members of a complex and ancient fertility dance venerating the ancient goddess of lavender?

OUR HATED REALITY
In a very short time you realize that no. The dancers on the poster are mostly citizens of the People's Republic of China. And female. They are taking photos in impossible positions, dressed in very elegant dresses of flowing linen, protected from the sun by raffia hats and lace umbrellas.

They are delicate and white like consumptive ladies of the camellias. They seem to be on the verge of staining their embroidered handkerchiefs with bloody flowers while decadent poets write about them and the immortal beauty they will achieve in exchange for the stumble of dying young.

HE
In my mind you will always be so beautiful.

SHE
Yes my life, but this could have already caught me in the good time of vaccines.

They evoke a frozen and romantic image of Europe. They seem to embody a golden time between Victorian times and modernism, possibly crystallized in a very pure way in steampunk manga. And they also seem to do it without any kind of modesty or irony. In fact, they are having a great time.

You are a guy raised in the nineties and, to be honest, this is all a bit over you. Your aesthetic culmination is PJ Harvey hugging Nick Cave while singing a murder ballad. Your aesthetic culmination is the Lost Highway by David Lynch. Your aesthetic culmination is Stray Toasters.

HOW DO YOU FACE THIS?
There are several ways to take the experience. Some include medication, no doubt. I propose the modest, although not the easiest: you stop the car on a wide shoulder, go down with your couple and your offspring and go into the fields to take pictures of yourself doing poses.

The thing will start with irony, at least you, sure, but, little by little, something will be born inside you. Something precious, naive and enormously superficial: a chewing gum and pastry happiness, a happiness of cupcake, of muffin and icing, of cappuccino foam in the mustache and umbrella of Cherbourg. And you will discover that tourists are the true heroes of our time.

Anyone can be a sensible traveler allergic to running water and fascinated by the real pulse of Mumbai's life; but it takes a blind will to put everyday horror aside and pose in a field of smelly lavender at almost ninety degrees of temperature, in the middle of nowhere, as if there were no tomorrow.

You have a panama and a flowered shirt somewhere in your closet. Use them to be a tourist, burn the back of your neck, stand in line for hours to see random monuments in the distance. To take pictures in huge fields of lilac flowers.

And then get in the car and get out of there like a soul carried by the devil, without getting stop by any of the inhabitants of the place. Somehow sensing that they wait at sunset, when all the tourists have already left, to take the places and take photos in impossible positions, like stuffed flamingos, like amber fossils.

Photos that they keep secret and observe with envy of those inhabitants of an absurd and better world.

IS IT A ROAD
OR AN AMUSEMENT PARK?

What if we asked an engineer dedicated to designing roller coasters to build us a road? Well, the truth is that I do not know exactly, but it is possible that the result was something similar to the Norwegian Atlantic Road.

Cataloged as a National Tourist Route, the tour allows us to enjoy coastal landscapes, culture and history, with various places of interest to visit and a varied fauna. But what really matters to us now is the road itself and its shapes, not capricious but necessary, which led it, in 2005, to win the award for Best Norwegian Construction of the 20th century, both for its design and for its functionality.

This baroque road, only about 8 kilometers long, connects the towns of Kristiansund and Molde, and it would be nothing special if it weren't for the fact that the former is on the mainland and the latter on the island of Averoy. That's right, the road runs above the sea. And you will tell me "Well, up to there it is nothing to write home about, nor is it a work that cannot be done with large steel columns well anchored to the ocean floor." And you would be right. But this is not the case.

GIVE ME TEN POINTS OF SUPPORT
AND I WILL MAKE YOU A ROAD

The architects saw that between the mainland and the island stood ten islands and decided that these would be their support points where the road would rest. Hey friend! And that's where the whims of nature come in and its mania for not making straight lines: impossible curves, hanging bridges, ups and downs ... A roller coaster to do by car and with the whole family, with a free ticket (until 1999 you had to pay toll) and with an approximate duration of 30 minutes, although those who take this road for the first time need much more time.

The islands are linked by eight bridges, the highest and most spectacular is the Storseisundet, 23 meters above sea level. Seen from far away, it looks like a road floating in the sky, twisting and bending over itself to plummet into a sea that is raging at times, calm at others, but always cold. An architecture that gives

another meaning to what bridge and road engineering students would call an easy-to-drive highway.

DO NOT BLIND THE ROAD
Throughout its entire route, there are numerous
rest points where you can stop the vehicle and enjoy the impressive views that the Hustadvika Strait
offers us to the Kvernesfjord and Freifjord fjords. A
changing landscape depending on the time of year we
decide to visit the Atlantic Road.

With radiant sun we can see whales and seals
in their natural habitat, as well as many species of
birds. But it is said that the best time of the year to
travel along this spectacular road is in autumn, with
much less benign weather. The reason is that on
stormy days and with strong wind, the waves cras-
hing against the bridges make the foam jump and fill
us with drops of water and saltpeter in a spectacle
worthy of the God of Thunder himself. Of course, it
reduces the speed that approach curves, wet floors
and poor visibility. Drama and beauty come together
in equal parts in the spectacle that is created when
nature fights against the wonders of man.

WE ARE HARD, WE ARE VIKINGS
The Norwegians are proud of this architectural
work of art and like to tell (we could say chulele) that
those who built this route had to see up to 12 hurrica-
nes during its construction. And it is that the project
began to take shape in 1909 and it was not until July 7,
1983 that it was completed. Even so, it was not under

construction all this time (I know, there are countries in which public works last longer, but I do not like to point the finger ...), but rather, as not only in Mediterranean countries, palace things They go slowly (am I pointing too much?), construction began in 1977.

Currently, the time when it is most used is in July, when the Molde Jazz Festival is held, which brings together thousands of people. Meanwhile, the locals are dedicated to fishing from the bridges, and the area is rich in fish, especially the exquisite cod.

An impossible road in the middle of exuberant and extreme nature. The ideal place to test any construction and the best cars in the shooting phase. Does anyone give more? Do we put wild boars crossing the lanes and some girls in the Nordic curves to liven up the journey?

FROM SACRED FOREST
TO PARK OF MONSTERS

I'm going to tell you one thing, like this, in petit committee: no one has ever had a clear reason for doing anything. Things happen, one is hooked or not to the train of events and that's it.

Or maybe it all starts with a joke, or with a temporal idea of first class or third regional. One comments at a dinner, almost in passing, that you would like to have a giant aviary in the garden, with pink macaws inside, and the next day your brother-in-law is already in the pet store preparing everything for your birthday. And of course, after blowing out the candles and before the talk about macaw care (I anticipate you: like all pets, they need more care than a Persian prince) you can't say "no, man no, it was really a joke. I like animals stuffed, on TV or grilled.

LET'S GO TO OURS

Pier Francesco Orsini was a noble condottier of the Italian Renaissance. He is usually represented holding a glass with a snake writhing inside it, a sign that is sometimes taken as death by poisoning and, at other times, as "he did unbelievable things when he was pimping." The second interpretation is more interesting to us, because one night the guy said strange things while he was drinking and after a few days some people were setting up a garden for him.

Drinking heavily was not uncommon between human beings in the 16th century. The water wasn't ionized at that time and it was more convenient to plug in wine, beer and other things, which were at least fermented. Also, the job as a condottier was stressful in itself. One cannot spend his life to commanding armies of mercenaries capable of changing sides in the middle of the battle and dedicated to the noble art of war (When the condottier said to his wife: "Honey, I finish my coffee and I start to work? Well, that) without some post-traumatic stress, which together with alcoholism and the brutality of feudal society, creates a vicious circle.

The fact is that, one night, Orsini, who had just lost his wife and was downcast, it came to his mind the idea to say to his trusted architect: "You are going to put me a garden with crazy monstrous statues, a total funeral roll. One thing to create tremendous bass and unparalleled horror, with giant turtles, crooked houses, elephants, mermaids, dragons, a huge face with a grotto in its mouth and every huge and disheveled mallet. And you do it to me in zero coma, because the oven is not for buns or the chirri for thunder".

NOTE: the translation from Florentine is free, but the background is more or less like this.

And since God does not cough up a condottier, after a few months the architect arrives and tells Orsini that he already has his Sacred Forest, the name does the thing, created. He comments that it is ravishing, paradoxical, ghostly and full of a strange beauty born of disproportion.

Orsini, who does not remember asking for a garden, visits him and resigns himself, but tells the architect to build a temple in honor of his new wife, who does not know how he is going to manage to tell him about the monsters.

WIFE
What's up, Condo?

CONDOTTIER
Very low, a lot. Go, bring a prisoner to execute, to see if I make the afternoon.

So Orsini ended up leaving for posterity a garden of enormous monsters near the town of Bomarzo, Viterbo.

There are a long thirty of monumental and mysterious statues: furies, sphinxes, dragons, bears, giant tortoises and much more. It highlights a crooked house and a monstrous face whose mouth houses a cave with table and chairs. And there is a nice temple just to compensate.

Now it can be visited, in fact, it is the main attraction of the town, but the place has been left for four hundred years. There is a photo, which I hope is true, that shows a shepherd leaning into the mouth of the monstrous face, with the flock of sheep undaunted and apart from the strangeness of the moment.

Ok, so much of what is said here is false. The garden exists, of course, but the story of the condottier is different.

THE FICTION OF FICTION

Manuel Mújica Laínez was an Argentine novelist who seemed to belong to the Sherlock Holmes dog series. He wrote a novel about the garden, entitled Bomarzo, where he tells that Pier Francesco Orsini was a hunchback, deviant and cynical, rough as a rice cake and, in general, a bad person, but with a little heart. His monstrosity ends up in the garden, a kind of autobiography that you can walk through.

Ah, but the fact is that, again, Mujica also invent almost everything. Neither Orsini was hunchbacked or deviant, nor, in general, any of that. He was a nice and handsome guy and it is not very clear what led him to create the garden. Not that Mujica tried to strain it doubled or anything like that. He said that he was making it up, but the legend has passed better to posterity than reality.

The fact is that there are some beautiful statues, if yours are the ruins. Occultists see messages in them. Dalí and Cocteau visited them and saw surrealism in them (Dalí painted a picture that is exhibited in the same garden). Mujica saw the life of a decadent dandy in them.

In short, only huge stones partially eaten by moss. You put the meaning, there and you eat it with your bread.

A TUNNEL IS NOT A PLACE FOR LOVE, IS IT?

When we think of romantic places we think of a beach at sunset, a walk under the stars, beds lined with freshly cut rose petals, dinners by candlelight, fireplaces and blankets in winter ... But what we do not think is in tunnels. At least in the tunnels we know full of smoke, soot and cars, without oxygen and with little light.

A ranking published by a dating portal said that the most romantic cities in the world, from 10 to 1 were: Prague, Florence, Dubrovnik, Budapest, Buenos Aires, Bruges, Kyoto, Venice, Sydney and, of course, Paris. City up, city down, surely you agree with each one of them. And many already live off their fame and have a multitude of activities for couples or, failing that, they sell that love is in the air (as John Paul Young sang) and that you will not leave without a deep, sincere and lasting infatuation. .

In short, they already say that marketing is the art of deceiving without being noticed.

But what if I told you that the only and unrepeatable tunnel of love is not in any of these majestic cities but in a small population of 8,000 inhabitants in Ukraine, what would you think? And if I also told you that couples who cross their tracks and make a wish come true, would you believe me? I know, maybe I wouldn't either, but I will try to convince you that one of the most romantic corners of the planet is located in one of the countries with the least influx of tourists in the world (it is at number 30 of the most visited).

THE TRAIN THAT CREATED LOVE

Kevan is a small town located in western Ukraine. A railway line connects the city with various wood processing factories. Right, at the moment more than a romantic comedy it looks like the beginning of a horror movie or the Slavic remake of Twin Peaks (that sawmill was scary). But don't worry, let's delve a little deeper into the subject.

The train was, and still is, the route through the forest. (Attention, a fable begins) As nobody cared for it, once the tracks were built, the vegetation grew again and claimed what was her: that part that was now marked by two long and thick metal guides. The train, for its part, struggled not to lose that terrain that it had gained from the forest and, after many battles, they reached a deal: nature allowed the iron horse to pass with the only condition that it let its around. (End of the fable).

In other words: the train did not allow vegetation to grow in the space it occupied in its multiple routes, breaking the small branches that could grow. In this way, was created a rectangular vegetable tunnel (the same as the railway) of about 3 kilometers in length. Nobody takes care of trimming it or caring for it, just the three trips that the train still makes each day allow this tunnel of love to continue to maintain its shape and, therefore, its charm.

THE SEASONS AND THE SUN

Spring, Summer, Autumn, Winter. Each season gives its particular charm to this unusual place. The ocher of the deciduous leaves, the green of the flowering, the white of the snow ... A constantly changing landscape that leaves no one indifferent who walks through its interior, away from the world, as in an earth worm hole that you do not know to what time or to what place it will take you.

But it is not only the seasons that modify the image of this wonder, but also the hours of the day, that is, depending on how the sun hits the leaves and allows it to enter through the small slits that remain between them. When the sun is high, the plants breathe a brilliant green, with clean, clear light. When it is low, the tunnel transforms into an enchanted forest, with dim lights that give the feeling that at any moment Little Red Riding Hood and the Wolf, Hansel and Grettel or good old Jason from Friday the 13th will appear.

MAKE A WISH

Thousands of couples allow themselves to be embraced by its attentive branches, but always prudent and distant, which take us away from civilization and transport us to other times, of great dresses and corsets, of hats and suits, of men and women. A dream that wakes up with the screeching of the train that warns us that we must move away in order to enjoy the love that is locked there, it has to do his tireless gardener work.

Like any good enchanted or charming place, this one also has its own legend that grants it supernatural powers that go beyond current human beliefs and unites it with the mystical world of fairies, goblins and ancient gods. In this case, the legend says that if a couple crosses the tracks and makes a wish, it will come true.

We do not know if it is true or not, what we know for sure is that our train would never stopped passing in order to continue enjoying the Klevan Tunnel of Love show.

Don't forget to say goodbye!

And well-born is also saying goodbye. Therefore, see you soon dear reader. I hope you have enjoyed. Don't forget to leave a review on Amazon and visit www.lais-ladelosconejos.com (I won't repeat trying to click on the link if it's a paper book).

Made in the USA
Middletown, DE
07 December 2020

26488649R00073